What I Wish Every Mom Would Ask Me:

Questions to Ask

Your Child's Doctor

at Every Visit

by Gary C. Morchower, M.D.

To my children, Andrew and Karen,
and to my wife, Bette, the best mom of them all.

Design by Peri Poloni.
Photography by Judy Nordseth
Baby model: Jacob Bayouth

ISBN 0-9720667-0-5

Contents

Part 1:
Newborn Disorders *(Diagnosed in the Hospital)*

Part 2:
Disorders of the General Pediatric and Adolescent Population

Part 3:

Choosing a Pediatrician

Why I Wrote This Book:

A Message to Every Mom Who's Ever Taken a Child to the Doctor

How many times have you returned with your child from the pediatrician's office, only to realize that you remember little of what was said to you during the visit? Perhaps it was because your mind was numb from having stayed up late the night before taking care of your sick child, or maybe you were so worried about your child's illness that you could only focus on a few things that were discussed during the visit. Maybe you just accept that your doctor is knowledgeable, and the only issue of concern to you now is that your child gets better.

If any of these scenarios sounds familiar, you are not alone. In my 32 years of practice, I've seen medicine change dramatically, and that has impacted the type, length and tenor of the pediatric office visit. Traditionally, families stayed with the same pediatrician throughout childhood, so they became comfortable with each other over the years. Now, with the emergence of managed care, families may change doctors as often as their employers change insurance plans. This can result in a game of "musical doctors," with the parent having to adapt to the styles, routines and personalities of different doctors all too frequently.

Also, in the past, parents often relied on a helpful nurse to explain everything after the doctor left the room and answer questions that came up. Now, nurses are just as busy as doctors, and it's less likely that you'll develop any better relationship with them, as you may see different nurses or nurse assistants at every office visit.

Perhaps the biggest change, though, is the length of the office visit. Doctors nowadays are more pressed for time than ever. Once they've established the appropriate diagnosis, they frequently deliver the treatment plan quickly, bombarding the parent with information. Consequently, the mom leaves the office with only a vague idea of what is going on.

Adding to the problem is that moms are often leery of questioning medical advice. Questions that should be asked often don't get asked. As a result, important areas of concern are not addressed — or worse, the treatment is misinterpreted or misunderstood.

Too often, I've heard parents say, "You mean he was supposed to finish the medicine even though he was feeling better?" or "I didn't know I was supposed to bring little Sarah back for a re-check," or "I thought I was to continue giving my child only clear liquids until the diarrhea had completely cleared."

The consequences of these misunderstandings may be minimal in some cases, but other times, the result is a recurrence of the original illness or the development of a complication.

I wrote this book because I don't want that to happen to your child. I want you to feel like you can ask your doctor questions even if you think they might seem silly. It's critical that you understand your child's condition fully and that you have all the information you need to help your child get better.

The book is organized into three parts: The first deals with conditions specific to newborns — those that show up at birth or in the hospital. The second consists of the most common conditions experienced by the general pediatric and adolescent population. Finally, there is a section on questions to ask when choosing a pediatrician. The book is organized alphabetically by disease, with a series of questions listed for each condition. Why just questions and no answers? Because it's important for your doctor to give the answers that are specific to your child's particular situation. You don't need to become a physician to help your child get better, you just need to know the right questions to ask.

I hope you'll bring this book with you to every office visit. Use it after the doctor has given you the diagnosis and formal treatment plan. If you forget or get distracted, call back later, book in hand, and use the questions to fill in the blanks of your understanding. There's plenty of space for you to take notes, so you have something to refer to when the memory of the doctor's verbal commentaries has faded.

How will your doctor feel about your newfound inquisitiveness? Many moms worry that questions such as these might irritate or alienate the doctor. I couldn't disagree more! WHEN IT COMES TO CARING FOR YOUR SICK CHILD, YOU HAVE EVERY RIGHT TO ASK WHATEVER QUESTIONS YOU NEED TO CLARIFY WHAT THE ILLNESS IS AND HOW YOU SHOULD TREAT IT.

In reality, the questions in this book are meant to complement the office visit and will only enhance the effectiveness of what the doctor is trying to accomplish. Most pediatricians want parents to leave with as much knowledge about the child's illness as possible. Indeed, it is my sincere hope that this book will enhance the relationship between you and your child's doctor, and that you have many productive and healthy visits down the road for years to come.

Part 1:

Newborn Disorders
(Diagnosed in the Hospital)

Arm Paralysis *(Brachial Plexus Palsy)*

Paralysis or weakness of the arm muscles.

1. How did this condition occur?

2. Is my baby experiencing any discomfort?

3. What tests need to be done to further define the condition?

4. What is the treatment, and will physical therapy be needed?

5. How long will it take for the condition to be corrected, and will there be any residual weakness or decreased function of the arm?

6. Should a neurologist or an orthopedist be consulted?

7. When do you wish to see my baby again for this condition?

Blood Infection *(Bacterial Sepsis)*

A serious condition caused by multiplying bacteria in the bloodstream.

1. What causes this condition?

2. What problems does it pose?

3. What tests need to be done to further define the condition?

4. How is this illness treated?

5. Do we need to consult with a neonatologist (new-born specialist) or an infectious disease specialist?

6. How long will it take for my baby to recover from this illness?

7. Will this condition weaken my baby in any way in the future, and will there be any long-term ill effects caused by it?

8. How long will my baby have to stay in the hospital as a result of this disorder?

9. Following discharge, what kind of follow-up will be needed?

Chromosomal Abnormalities

Abnormalities in the genetic makeup of the child that can manifest in structural and mental ways.

1. What features does my baby have that make you suspect this kind of disorder?

2. How did my baby develop this type of condition?

3. What tests need to be done to further define the disorder?

4. What kind of impairments can occur as a result of this condition?

5. Is this disorder treatable?

6. Is it possible that any of our future children might be born with this disorder?

7. Do we need to consult with a geneticist or any other specialist?

8. What kind of special plans should be made with regard to caring for the baby once we arrive home?

9. When do you wish to see my baby again for this condition?

Clubfoot

Deformities of the foot.

1. What caused this condition to occur?

2. What exactly is structurally wrong with the foot?

3. How is it treated, and how successful is the treatment?

4. Will my child be able to walk and exercise normally following treatment?

5. Do you think that there will be any limitations or disadvantages athletically because of this condition?

6. When do we need to see an orthopedic surgeon?

7. Following discharge, what kind of follow-up with you will be needed for this condition?

Heart Disease — Congenital

Heart or conduction system abnormalities that occur at birth.

1. What is wrong with my baby's heart, and what problems does the defect cause?

2. Is the condition potentially dangerous?

3. What tests need to be done to further define the condition?

4. Will my baby need surgery, and is the condition correctable?

5. Will any heart medicines be needed to treat this problem?

6.   If medicines are used, what potential side effects do we need to look for?

7. Do we need to see a pediatric cardiologist and, if so, when?

8. Will my baby become blue (cyanotic) from this condition?

9. After I leave the hospital, what danger signs do I look for that would indicate my baby is having a problem related to this condition?

10. Do I need to limit my baby's activities in any way after we go home?

11. Following discharge, when do you wish to see my baby again concerning this condition?

Hypoglycemia

Low blood sugar.

1. What caused this condition?

2. Is this condition dangerous, and will it have any permanent impact on my baby's health?

3. What tests need to be done to further define the condition?

4. How are we going to treat it, and are there any side effects that might occur from the treatments?

5. How long will the condition take to correct?

6. Is there a chance the condition might recur following discharge, and is there any special need for follow-up?

7. Does this condition predispose my baby to developing diabetes or any other sugar metabolism disorder later in life?

8. Will future babies that I might have be more inclined to have this disorder, and is there any precaution that I might take to prevent it from happening again?

9. Following discharge, when do you wish to see my baby again for this condition?

Hypospadius

When the opening normally at the end of the penis is located on the undersurface of the penis.

1. What caused this condition?

2. What tests need to be done to further define the condition?

3. What kind of symptoms or problems can occur as a result of it?

4. Will it need to be corrected — if so, when and how?

5. Do we need to see a urologist and, if so, when?

6. Is there a possibility that there will be a problem later on in sexual or urinary function?

7. Following discharge, when do you wish to see my child again for this condition?

Intestinal Inflammation
(Necrotizing Enterocolitis)

An acute inflammation of the inner lining of the bowel with the presence of membrane-like areas and superficial ulceration.

1. What caused this condition?

2. What tests need to be done to further define the condition?

3. What potential dangers does this disorder pose?

4. What is the treatment for this disorder, and how long will it take for my baby to recover?

5. Are there any potential side effects of the treatment?

6. Is it possible that this condition could get worse?

7. Do we need to consult a neonatologist (newborn specialist) or gastroenterologist?

8. Will I be able to breastfeed my baby during this illness?

9. Following discharge, what kind of follow-up will be needed?

Jaundice

Yellow appearance of the skin caused by bile pigment deposits in the skin.

1. What is jaundice, and what caused it to appear in my baby?

2. Is the condition dangerous?

3. What tests need to be done to further define the condition?

4. What is considered to be a danger point for the bilirubin level?

5. If my baby's bilirubin level exceeds that point, what kind of therapy will be indicated and will it correct the problem?

6. Is this type of therapy safe, and will there be any bad consequences or repercussions afterwards?

7. How often do we follow the bilirubin level, and will we continue to follow the level at home following discharge?

8. Can my baby become anemic from this disorder?

9. Is there anything else we need to know concerning this condition and its management?

10. Following discharge, what kind of follow-up will be needed?

Kidney Enlargement *(Hydronephrosis)*

Swelling of the kidney as a result of obstruction to the flow or urine.

1. What caused this condition?

2. What tests are needed to further define the disorder?

3. Is this condition causing my baby any pain or discomfort?

4. Is it correctable, and will surgery be necessary?

5. Will it predispose my baby to kidney disease or infection in the future?

6. Do we need to consult a urologist and, if so, when?

7. How will the condition be monitored following discharge, and what tests will need to be done?

8. What danger signs should we look for after leaving the hospital that would indicate that the kidney problem might be getting worse?

9. Following discharge, when do you wish to see my baby again?

Lung Rupture
(Pneumothorax or Pneumomediastinum)

Free air in the chest cavity.

1. What caused this condition?

2. How is it treated?

3. How long will it take to correct itself?

4. Do we need to consult with a neonatologist (newborn specialist) or a pediatric surgeon?

5. What tests need to be done to further define the condition?

6. What kind of future complications can we anticipate as a result of this illness?

7. Are the lungs left weakened from this condition and, if so, in what way?

8. Following discharge, what kind of follow-up will be needed?

Meconium Aspiration

When the newborn or fetus inhales meconium (first stool) into the lower respiratory tract.

1. What caused this condition?

2. Is this condition dangerous, and what kind of damage can it cause?

3. What tests need to be done to further define the condition?

4. What is the treatment?

5. What side effects can occur from the treatment?

6. How long will it take for my baby to show improvement?

7. What complications can develop?

8. Can pneumonia develop?

9. Will this condition weaken my baby's lungs for the future?

10. Following discharge, what kind of follow-up will be needed?

Pneumonia — Neonatal

An infection of the lungs that prevents them from functioning properly.

1. What caused this condition?

2. How dangerous is this condition, and what complications can occur?

3. What is the proposed treatment?

4. What potential side effects can occur from the treatment?

5. How long will it take for my baby to improve once treatment has begun?

6. What additional diagnostic tests should my baby have?

7. After my baby gets better, will he be more prone to respiratory tract infections in the future?

8. Do we need to consult with a neonatologist (new-born specialist) or a pulmonologist?

9. What kind of follow-up will be needed with you in the future pertaining to this condition?

Rapid Breathing
(Respiratory Distress Syndrome/Transient Tachypnea)

Rapid breathing in the early days of life due to to immaturity of the lungs or decreased absorption of fetal lung fluid.

1. What caused this condition?

2. What is actually taking place in the lungs?

3. How does it differ from pneumonia?

4. What tests need to be done to further define this condition?

5. How dangerous is this condition, and can we expect a complete recovery?

6. What kind of treatment will be needed, and are there any potential bad side effects from the treatment?

7. How long will my baby need to stay in the hospital?

8. Will the treatment or the disorder weaken the lungs in the future and predispose my baby to future respiratory tract problems?

9. Will I be able to stay in the hospital until my baby is fully recovered?

10. Will any treatment be needed at home following discharge and, if so, who will help me administer it?

11. Do we need to consult with a neonatologist (newborn specialist) or a pulmonary specialist?

12. Is this hospital capable of dealing with this disorder or does my baby need to be transferred to another hospital that is more capable of dealing with difficult illnesses?

13. Following discharge, what kind of follow-up will be needed?

Scalp Swelling *(Cephalohematoma)*

A swelling of the scalp caused by a hemorrhage under the outer layer of bone in one area of the skull.

1. What caused this condition?

2. Is it potentially dangerous?

3. Does it represent any possible injury to the brain?

4. What tests need to be done to further define the condition?

5. Are there any other potential problems that can occur in the future?

6. How long will it take for this condition to get better?

7. How often will you need to see my baby for follow-up of this condition after discharge from the hospital?

Seizures *(Neonatal)*

Convulsive fits or spasms during the first month of life.

1. What causes this condition?

2. How are they treated, and how effective is the treatment?

3. Are there any side effects to the medicines used in the treatment?

4. What potential harm can the seizures have, and can they cause brain damage?

5. What tests do we need to do to establish any possible underlying cause?

6. Do you think the seizures will recur, and what are the possibilities that my baby will outgrow them?

7. Do we need to consult with a neurologist?

8. Are there any precautions we need to take when we go home, such as connecting my baby to an apnea monitor?

9. When do you wish to see my child again regarding this condition following discharge?

Undescended Testicle(s)

When one or both testicles do not descend completely into the sac.

1. What causes this condition?

2. Is there a danger of sterility or any other problem as a result of this condition?

3. Will an operation be necessary to correct this condition and, if so, when?

4. When do we need to consult a surgeon?

5. Are there any medicines that can be used to help bring down the testicle(s)?

6. Are there any danger signs I should look for?

7. Following discharge, when do you wish to see my baby again for this condition?

Part 2:

Disorders of the General Pediatric and Adolescent Population

Acne

A chronic inflammatory disease of the sebaceous glands characterized by pimples and pustules occurring primarily on the face and back.

There is no need for acne to cause severe scarring. Today there are good treatments that can minimize the long-term cosmetic ill effects caused by this condition.

1. What causes this condition?

2. Is there any way to predict how bad it will get?

3. What can I do to prevent it from getting worse?

4. Does diet affect it?

5. What skin cleanser should be used?

6. What about topical antibiotics and Retin A?

7. What about oral antibiotics?

8. Is it bad enough to consider the use of oral retinoic acid (Accutane)?

9. If any of these medicines are used, how long should they be taken and what are the potential side effects?

10. When should we consider seeing a dermatologist?

11. When do you want to see my child again regarding this condition?

Anemia

A condition of reduced red blood cells in the circulatory system.

We worry about anemia because it can make children sluggish and decrease their capacity to perform. There is no reason, though, why the cause of anemia cannot be fully established and appropriate treatment rendered, if necessary.

1. What causes this condition?

2. What tests need to be done to better define the condition?

3. How is it treated, and is it correctable?

4. Are there any potential side effects of the treatment?

5. What symptoms will my child manifest as a result of the condition?

6. Do we need to consult a hematologist (blood disorder specialist)?

7. How often will my child need to be tested in the future to see if the condition is improving?

8. When do you wish to see my child again regarding this disorder?

Appendicitis

Inflammation of the appendix in the large intestine.

Whenever a child complains of severe abdominal pains you might worry that the child may have appendicitis. If abdominal pain develops suddenly and the child continues to complain, you should call your doctor. It is important that this condition be diagnosed early to avoid having the appendix rupture, which causes more serious problems for the child.

1. How did my child develop appendicitis?

2. Are there further tests to be done to more fully establish the diagnosis?

3. What is the treatment for this condition?

4. What complications can occur as a result of this condition if left untreated?

5. What, where, and by whom should the surgery to correct this condition be performed?

6. If surgery is indicated, what are the potential complications that can subsequently occur?

7. When do you wish to see my child again regarding this condition?

Asthma

A disorder characterized by spasms and inflammation of the bronchial tubes resulting in wheezing.

Fortunately, there are many new treatments available today to better treat and prevent asthma flare-ups. With proper medical supervision, children's lives and physical activities do not have to be handicapped by this condition nearly as much as they were in the past.

1. What is the cause of this disorder, and how did my child develop it?

2. Is it hereditary?

3. What is the natural course of the disease?

4. How does infection play a role?

5. How is the condition treated, and what are the potential complications of the treatment?

6. Are there long-term problems that can occur as a result of this disorder?

7. What tests are needed to substantiate the disorder and to determine the severity of an episode?

8. How are further flare-ups of this condition prevented?

9. Is it necessary to purchase a breathing machine for home use?

10. What are the chances of my child outgrowing this condition?

11. What symptoms or signs do I need to look for that would indicate my child is getting worse during an episode?

12. Do we need to see a pulmonary or asthma specialist?

13. What kind of follow-up is needed for this condition?

Athlete's Foot *(Tinea Pedis)*

Fungal infection of the foot.

There's no need to have your little athlete's feet itching and burning all the time. With proper medical management, this condition can be effectively treated and controlled.

1. What is the cause of this condition, and how did my child develop it?

2. Is it contagious?

3. What medicines are used to treat this condition, and how long are they to be taken?

4. What are the potential side effects of these medicines?

5. When would you expect the symptoms to subside?

6. How long will it take to cure the condition?

7. How do we prevent it from spreading to other people?

8. What can we do to prevent it from coming back?

9. What reasons would warrant my calling you back regarding my child's condition?

10. When do you wish to see my child again for this condition?

Attention Deficit Disorder

A disorder characterized by an inability to stay focused and attentive.

This condition, alarmingly, is being diagnosed in epidemic proportions in the pediatric population. Be sure there is firm evidence for the diagnosis before you embark on a treatment plan. It is important that you keep in close communication with your child's teacher and doctor to get the best possible outcome for your child.

1. What causes this disorder?
2. Is it hereditary or environmental?
3. What medicines are used to treat this condition?
4. What are the potential side effects of the prescribed medicine?
5. Should my child take the medicine on weekends?
6. Is the medicine dangerous in any way to use for long periods of time?
7. Are there alternative methods of treatment other than medicine?
8. What are the chances of my child outgrowing this condition and when?
9. Are there any other aspects of care that can be helpful in making this condition better?
10. Do I need to take my child to a psychologist or a neurologist?
11. How can the school help?
12. When do I report back to you concerning my child's progress?
13. How often will you need to see my child in the future regarding this condition?

Back Pain

Backaches in childhood can sometimes be more serious than a muscle strain. If the symptom persists, have it thoroughly evaluated by your child's doctor.

1. What are the possible causes for this condition?

2. What tests can be done to better define the cause of the problem, and is now the right time to perform these tests?

3. What can be done to make the condition better?

4. Are there any medicines that can be used?

5. If medicine is used, what are the potential side effects?

6. What kind of exercise limitations should be enforced?

7. Do we need to consult with an orthopedist or a chiropractor?

8. When do you wish to see my child again for this problem?

Bedwetting *(Enuresis)*

Involuntary wetting of the bed.

This is frequently an embarrassing condition for children when they reach grade school age. Fortunately, once you have your child evaluated by the doctor, usually an effective treatment can be prescribed.

1. What causes this condition?

2. How long will it last?

3. Is there any treatment for this condition, and at what age should it begin?

4. How successful is the treatment?

5. Are there any side effects from the treatment?

6. What further diagnostic tests are indicated to better define the problem?

7. Could there be psychological factors involved?

8. Do we need to consult a urologist?

9. When do you wish to see my child again regarding this condition?

Bellyaches *(Recurrent Abdominal Pain)*

This is one of the most common complaints in childhood. If the symptom persists or is severe to the point of interfering with your child's daily activities, it warrants a complete evaluation by the doctor.

1. What are the possible causes for this condition?

2. What further tests need to be done to substantiate the diagnosis and to make sure this condition is not one that needs further attention?

3. Do you think the condition could be one that may require surgery?

4. Are there any medicines that can make the condition better?

5. If medicines are used to make the condition better, how long should they be taken, and what are the potential side effects?

6. How long do you think the abdominal discomfort will last?

7. What things do I look for that would suggest the condition is getting worse?

8. When should I call you back concerning my child's condition?

9. What kind of follow-up is needed?

Bellybutton Bulge *(Umbilical Hernia)*

A weakness in the tissues of the umbilicus permitting the abdominal contents to bulge out.

Though it may be unattractive, the belly-button "outie" poses no health problems and usually resolves on its own over a period of time.

1. What is the cause of this condition, and how did my child develop it?

2. What are the potential problems that can occur as a result of it?

3. What is the natural history of this condition if left untreated?

4. What is the treatment of this condition, and is surgery ever indicated?

5. If surgery is indicated, when, where, and by whom should the surgery be performed?

6. What are the potential complications that can occur as a result of the surgery?

7. When do you wish to see my child again for this condition?

Bladder Infection *(Cystitis)*

Infection of the bladder.

Make sure you do all the follow-ups and diagnostic tests your doctor recommends regarding this condition. You don't want this to lead to a chronic condition later on in life.

1. What causes this condition, and how did my child contract it?

2. Now that my child has this condition, what are the chances that it will recur?

3. What is the treatment for this condition, and how long will it be continued?

4. If medicines are used, what are the potential side effects that can be encountered?

5. How long will the symptoms last once treatment is started?

6. Are there any x-ray studies that need to be performed to determine if there is any underlying anatomical reason that led to this type of infection?

7. If there is an anatomical abnormality, will we need to see a urologist?

8. When do I need to bring in follow-up urine specimens to see if the medicines are working?

9. When should I call you back regarding this condition?

10. When do you wish to see my child again for a follow-up exam?

Blood in Urine (Hematuria)

Frequently, this condition is picked up as part of a routine well-check exam. It can represent a serious underlying condition, so be sure to do all the follow-up testing that your doctor requests.

1. What are the possible causes of this condition?

2. Are any of the causes potentially dangerous for my child?

3. Is there any specific treatment for this disorder, and are there any activity restrictions that need to be imposed?

4. What diagnostic tests should be done to better define the cause of this problem?

5. Will my child outgrow this condition?

6. Do we need to see a nephrologist or a urologist?

7. What symptoms pertaining to this condition would warrant my calling you back again?

8. How often do you want to test the urine for blood in the future?

9. When do you wish to see my child again regarding this condition?

Blood Vessel Birthmark *(Hemangioma)*

A superficial collection of blood vessels on the skin.

Most of these unsightly birthmarks fade significantly over a period of time. Keep in mind, however, that some get worse before they get better. Rarely, some of these do not regress to a desirable level and may require more aggressive action at a later date.

1. What causes this condition to occur, and how did my child acquire it?

2. Did something happen during the pregnancy that might have caused it?

3. Is it potentially dangerous?

4. What kind of treatment is indicated, or will it fade on its own?

5. Will it eventually leave a disfiguring mark?

6. Do we need to consult with a dermatologist regarding this condition?

7. What kind of follow-up is needed?

Boil *(Carbuncle)*

A painful nodular area of inflammation in the skin, frequently with a central core of pus.

Some children are more prone to developing boils than others. If your child falls into this category, pay more attention to the child's personal hygiene and talk to your doctor about what else can be done to prevent recurrences.

1. What causes this condition?

2. Is it contagious and, if so, how do I prevent it from spreading to other people?

3. What is the treatment?

4. If medicines are prescribed, how long should they be used?

5. Are there any complications or side effects that can occur as a result of the treatment?

6. How effective is the treatment in eradicating the condition?

7. What can be done to prevent a recurrence of this disorder?

8. What kind of follow-up is needed?

Breast Enlargement in Males *(Gynecomastia)*

Abnormal breast enlargement in a male.

This can be an embarrassing condition for children, especially for teenagers. It occurs in approximately one-third of teenage males. In most cases, straightforward information and reassurance go a long way in bolstering the child's self-esteem.

1. What causes this condition?

2. Is there something hormonally wrong with him?

3. What can be done to correct this condition?

4. Are there any tests that need to be done to further define the cause of this disorder?

5. Do you think the breasts will grow any larger?

6. How should I counsel my child?

7. Do we need to see any type of specialist for this condition?

8. When do you wish to see my child again regarding this condition?

Breath-Holding Spells

Periods of holding breath.

Witnessing your child holding his breath can be a frightening experience for parents, but the condition usually poses no serious threat for your child. It is important that you consult your child's doctor so that an accurate diagnosis can be established. These "spells" are age-related, and usually disappear by the time the child is five or six years old.

1. What is the cause of this condition?

2. How dangerous is this condition for my child, and what are the potential problems that can occur?

3. Is this condition a type of seizure?

4. What diagnostic tests are indicated to further define the cause or to rule out anything more serious?

5. Will my child outgrow this condition and, if so, when?

6. What is the best way to treat this condition if it occurs again?

7. Do we need to see a neurologist or psychologist?

8. When do you wish to see my child again for this condition?

Bronchiolitis

Inflammation of the small airway passages and surrounding tissue leading to the lungs seen in infants. It causes wheezing and sometimes labored breathing.

This respiratory illness can be a frightening condition for a parent to observe and to endure. It requires a great deal of vigilance and committed care on your part. You need to stay in close communication with the doctor and know what signs to look for to determine whether the condition is getting worse.

1. What is the cause of this condition, and how did my child contract it?

2. Is it contagious and, if so, what measures should be taken to prevent its spread?

3. How is this condition treated?

4. If medicines are prescribed, what are their potential side effects?

5. How does the condition differ from asthma?

6. What are the danger signs that we need to look for that might indicate that the treatment for this disorder is not progressing as well as it should?

7. What complications can develop from this disorder?

8. Now that my child has had this condition, does it mean that it will occur over and over again?

9. How long does it usually take for a child with this condition to show improvement?

10. When do you wish to see my child again for follow-up of this disorder?

Bronchitis

Infection of larger air tubes leading to the lungs.

What is frequently referred to as bronchitis in childhood is generally a more diffuse respiratory tract condition involving more than just the bronchial tubes. Recurrent episodes of this condition warrant a more thorough diagnostic work-up.

1. What is the cause of this condition, and how did my child contract it?

2. What complications can occur from this condition?

3. How is it treated?

4. What are the potential side effects that can occur from the treatment?

5. Is the condition contagious and, if so, for how long?

6. What restrictions should be placed on my child because of the condition?

7. When can my child return to school and resume physical activity?

8. What symptoms should I look for that would cause me to call you back again?

9. When do you wish to see my child again for this condition?

Bruising (Excessive)

Areas of discoloration caused by superficial injury to the skin without laceration

Bruising on the legs is common in childhood and part of growing up. Bruising that is more widely distributed over the body is more worrisome, and you should consult your child's doctor for possible evaluation.

1. What causes this bruising?

2. Is the bruising my child exhibits normal or could there be an underlying problem in the blood that exists?

3. Do we need to do any tests to determine more specifically what is causing the bruising?

4. Would any vitamins or medicine be of help?

5. Do we need to consult with a hematologist?

6. Are there any danger signs I need to look for?

7. Do you need to see my child again regarding this condition?

Chicken Pox *(Varicella)*

An acute contagious infection with pock marks on the skin, fever, and a general feeling of malaise.

Thank heavens, the varicella vaccine has reduced the incidence of this disease considerably. Nonetheless, even if your child has had the vaccine, it can still occur. If it does, though, it will likely be a much milder case.

1. What causes this condition?

2. How is it spread, and how long will my child be contagious?

3. How long has my child been contagious prior to the appearance of the pox lesions?

4. If another person was exposed to my child and contracted the disease, how long would it take for that person to eventually break out with the pox lesions?

5. If you have had this disease once, can you contract it again?

6. How is it treated and for how long?

7. What complications can occur as a result of this disease?

8. Is there any way to shorten its course?

9. Will it leave any permanent scars?

10. Is there any way to prevent a person exposed to my child from coming down with the disease?

11. What kind of follow-up is needed?

Colic

Pronounced irritability in the first months of life.

This condition can cause mothers to feel helpless and depressed. I have always felt the best way for mothers to get through this difficult period is to stay in close contact with the doctor and have the infant checked and rechecked frequently for reassurance.

1. What causes colic?

2. How long is it supposed to last?

3. With a breastfeeding mother, is there anything in the diet that might contribute to the colic?

4. With a baby that is formula fed, does changing the formula to a soy or possibly a protein hydrolysate help?

5. What about medicines — do they help?

6. Is there anything else I can do to make my baby feel better?

7. How long should I let my baby cry, and does crying over a period of time harm the baby in any way?

8. Are there any tests that need to be done to make sure that the baby's irritability is nothing more serious than colic?

9. What signs or symptoms do I look for that would make me need to call you back?

10. When do you want to see my child again for this condition?

Constipation

Infrequency of bowel movements.

I am frequently called by parents about this condition. Once constipation persists for awhile, it can be self-perpetuating and can cause a great deal of concern in the family. Fortunately, there are effective ways of treating this condition at every age.

1. What causes constipation?

2. What are the potential problems that can arise from this condition?

3. How is it treated?

4. What are the potential side effects from the treatment?

5. Can diet play a role in the cause and/or treatment?

6. What further diagnostic tests are indicated?

7. *(If chronic)* Does my child need to see a gastrointestinal specialist?

8. What symptoms would cause me to call you back regarding this condition?

9. What kind of follow-up is needed in the future?

Corneal Abrasion

A scratch on the colored part of the eye (cornea).

This is a potentially serious occurrence and warrants close follow-up with your child's physician. Typically, though, this condition is usually healed in 48 hours.

1. What has actually occurred to my child's eye?

2. What potential dangers does this condition pose?

3. How is it treated and for how long?

4. Are there any side effects that can occur from the proposed treatment?

5. Do we need to see an ophthalmologist (eye specialist) and, if so, when?

6. When do you wish to see my child again in the future for this condition?

Cradle Cap *(Seborrheic Dermatitis)*

Inflammation and scaliness of the scalp and surrounding area.

This is a very common condition in infancy and is relatively easily treated. It may be confused with the more generalized condition of infantile eczema.

1. What causes this condition, and how did my child develop it?

2. How long will it last?

3. How does it differ from dandruff?

4. Can it get infected?

5. What is the treatment?

6. Are there any side effects of the treatment that can be anticipated?

7. How long does it take to get better?

8. What signs do I look for to call you back?

9. When do you wish to see my child again for this condition?

Crohns Disease *(Regional Ileitis)*

Inflammation primarily of the small intestine with resultant fever, diarrhea and weight loss.

This chronic intestinal condition can cause children hours of misery. However, it can be adequately treated, and usually, children can function normally.

1. What causes this disorder, and how did my child contract it?

2. What is the natural course of this disease over a long period of time?

3. Is the disorder hereditary, or are there environmental factors involved?

4. Does diet play a role?

5. What medicines are used to treat my child's disorder, and how long are they to be used?

6. How soon do the medicines take effect, and when will my child start getting better?

7. What are the potential side effects of the medicines?

8. Does surgery play a role in the treatment now or later on?

9. What signs do I look for to determine whether my child is getting worse?

10. Do I need to see a pediatric gastroenterologist?

11. What symptoms would warrant my calling you back?

12. How often do you wish to see my child regarding this condition?

Croup

Inflammation of the larynx resulting in a barking-type cough.

This can be a frightening disease for parents to watch as you see your child struggling to breathe. It requires a great deal of parental vigilance with close medical supervision. Though it may be a grueling period of time, the condition is usually much improved in two to three days. Nonetheless, once you have experienced this condition, you will never forget the sound of the high-pitched barking cough associated with it.

1. What causes this condition, and how did my child contract it?

2. Is it contagious and for how long?

3. What can be done to treat it?

4. Are antibiotics or steroids effective as part of the treatment and, if so, how long should they be used?

5. If used, what are the potential side effects from these medicines?

6. Are steroids effective in the treatment?

7. What are the potential complications of croup, and how will I recognize them?

8. What am I supposed to do if I encounter these complications?

9. Are there any specific precautions I should take with regard to my child's sleeping?

10. Should I sleep in the same room?

11. How long will it take for my child to show improvement?

12. When should I call you back again?

13. When do you wish to see my child again regarding this condition?

Cuts (Requiring Stitches)

Some cuts that required stitches by doctors in the past are now glued. Be sure to make your house as safe as possible . . . coffee tables and fireplace hearths are still prime offenders.

1. Will stitches be required to repair this cut?

2. Are there any treatment options available other than stitching?

3. Is the cut serious enough to require a plastic surgeon?

4. Will the cut leave a scar? If so, what can be done to minimize the scarring?

5. Are the stitches absorbable? If not, when do the stitches need to be taken out?

6. What signs do I look for that might indicate that the cut is getting infected?

7. Shall I leave the cut open or covered, and will it need a topical antibiotic?

8. What do I do to prevent my child from pulling out the stitches?

9. What physical limitations should I impose to protect the cut and for how long?

10. Does my child need a tetanus shot as a result of the cut?

11. When do you wish to see my child again to remove the stitches?

Developmental Delay

A delay in the area of physical or mental development.

If you or your physician suspect a developmental delay in your child, it's wise to see if your state has a public agency that will evaluate and provide treatment for these conditions. Early intervention is most important in addressing cognitive or motor areas when you suspect a delay.

1. What is the cause of this condition?

2. What kind of treatment is necessary, and how long will it take to see improvement?

3. What are the chances that, with treatment, these delays can be overcome, and what long-term results can we expect?

4. How much of a difference would it make if no treatment at all took place?

5. Does my child need to be evaluated by a neurologist or a developmental specialist?

6. What kind of follow-up will be needed with you in the future for this condition?

Diabetes *(Mellitus)*

A metabolic disorder that comes from a deficiency of insulin production in the pancreas, giving rise to elevated blood sugar.

This condition can be adequately regulated with good medical supervision, adherence to a strict diet, and daily insulin monitoring. I like the diabetic summer camps, which provide not only recreation, but diabetic education as well as a sense of camaraderie with kids that have the same disorder.

1. What causes this condition, and how did my child contract it?

2. What is the normal course of the disease, and where do I go for more education?

3. What medicines are used for treatment, and are there any potential side effects that can be encountered as a result of their usage?

4. What is the best way to regulate the dosage of the medication?

5. How big a role does diet play in the control and progression of the disease?

6. What signs do I look for to know if my child is getting in trouble with the disease?

7. Do we need to see an endocrinologist (diabetes specialist)?

8. Do my other children need to be tested for diabetes?

9. How often do I need to check back with you?

10. When do you wish to see my child again regarding this condition?

Diaper Rash

Rash in the diaper area.

Try one of the over-the-counter preparations first, and keep your infant's diaper area as dry as possible. If the condition does not improve, contact your doctor because it may represent a yeast infection or some other type of infection that requires a prescription medication to get better.

1. What causes this condition, and how did my child contract it?

2. Is it painful?

3. How contagious is it?

4. What is the treatment for this condition?

5. Are there any side effects from the treatment?

6. How long will the rash persist once appropriate treatment is instituted?

7. Will there be any scarring?

8. What can be done to prevent this condition from reoccurring?

9. When do you wish to see my child again for this condition?

Diarrhea

Increase in frequency and fluidity of stools.

Follow the directions you get from your doctor to make this condition improve. If the diarrhea persists, keep checking with the doctor because, although most diarrheas get better with simple dietary control, sometimes there can be an underlying cause that requires special treatment.

1. What is the cause of this condition, and how did my child contract it?

2. Are there any other tests to be done, such as a stool culture or a parasite test to further define the cause?

3. How long will the diarrhea last?

4. What is the treatment for this condition?

5. If I am to stop giving cow's milk to my child, when can I resume giving it?

6. If I am to put my child on a limited diet, when will I know to progress the diet back to normal?

7. Are there any medicines to be given to slow down the diarrhea and, if so, how long should they be used?

8. What are the potential side effects that can be incurred as a result of their usage?

9. What are the danger signs to look for if the diarrhea persists?

10. When do I call you back if the diarrhea continues?

11. Do you wish to see my child again regarding this condition?

Dysplasia of the Hip

Abnormal development of the hip.

This condition may not be present at birth and may be detected later on in infancy. This is one of the reasons you need to go back often for regular checkups during the first year of life. If detected early, this condition can often be completely corrected.

1. What is the actual problem with the hip, and why did it occur?

2. What is the treatment, and should an orthopedist be consulted at this time?

3. Is the condition totally correctable or is it likely that there will be a residual problem?

4. How long will it take for the prescribed treatment to correct this disorder?

5. What type of restrictions will need to be imposed upon my child because of the disorder and the treatment?

6. What kind of follow-up will be needed?

Ear Infection — Middle Ear *(Otitis Media)*

Infection of the middle ear.

Ear infections are common during the early years — so common that I once contemplated changing our practice name to "Ear Infections Are Us." It is important to follow up with your doctor after you have finished the treatment regimen to make sure that the infection, as well as the fluid in the middle ear, has sufficiently cleared.

1. What causes this condition, and how did my child develop it?

2. What medicines are needed to combat this infection?

3. What medicines can I give my child to relieve the pain?

4. Are there any side effects associated with the medicines used in the treatment of this condition?

5. After treatment has started, when should I see improvement?

6. What can be done to prevent this condition from recurring?

7. In the case of recurrent ear infections, when does the consideration of ventilatory tubes come into play, and when should we see an ENT specialist?

8. How can we be sure that there is no permanent hearing loss associated with this condition?

9. When do you wish to see my child again regarding this condition?

Ear Infection — Outer Ear *(Otitis Externa)*

Inflammation of the outer canal of the ear.

This is the so-called "Swimmer's Ear" type of ear infection. Despite the name, however, a lot of these external ear infections don't occur from swimming, but are caused when water from any source gets behind an accumulation of wax in the external ear resulting in inflammation and infection. Once your child has had "Swimmer's Ear," it is a good idea to use preventative drops whenever the child goes swimming.

1. What is the cause of this condition, and how did my child contract it?

2. What is the treatment for this condition, and how long should it be continued?

3. What are the potential side effects from the treatment?

4. How long will it take for the ear pain to subside?

5. When can my child resume putting his/her head under water?

6. What can be done to prevent this condition from recurring?

7. When do you wish to see my child again regarding this disorder?

Earwax Impaction *(Cerumen)*

Earwax lodged in and blocking the ear canal.

This is relatively common and, at times, is so severe that it can impair hearing and indirectly lead to external ear infections. It seems like every doctor has a different approach to dealing with this problem and removing the wax.

1. What causes this condition?

2. What can be done to make it better?

3. Does the condition impair my child's hearing?

4. What danger is created by leaving the wax alone, as is?

5. What is candling, and is it applicable for this disorder?

6. Are there any preventive measures that can be taken to prevent this condition from recurring?

7. What kind of follow-up is needed in the future?

Eating Disorder (i.e. Bulemia, Anorexia)

Pathologic disturbance of the eating pattern.

It seems that these types of disorders are becoming more and more prevalent, especially in our teenage population. It is a probable consequence of multiple factors, including family tendencies, peer pressure, school stress and our fast-paced society. A multi-pronged approach is needed for treatment.

1. What causes children to experience this kind of disorder?

2. What are some of the issues that need to be discussed and explored to further define the problem area?

3. How does one differentiate whether this is a phase, as opposed to a more serious long-term disorder?

4. Can depression be an underlying issue?

5. What can I do to make it better and to help my child overcome this disorder?

6. Is it necessary to consult a nutritionist?

7. Is the timing right to consult a psychologist or psychiatrist?

8. Is there any medication that can be used to help treat this condition?

9. Are there any side effects from the medicine?

10. How often does my child need to be weighed?

11. When do you wish to see my child again for this disorder?

Eczema

An inflammatory skin condition with itching, watery discharge at times, and the formation of scales and crusts.

This is a common skin condition in youngsters. Most will eventually outgrow it. In the meantime, keep using the lubricants, special skin cleansers and creams that your doctor prescribes.

1. What causes this condition?

2. Is it hereditary?

3. What are the different ways of treating this condition?

4. What medicines can be used to treat this disorder, and how long will it take for this condition to show improvement?

5. If used, are there any potential side effects from these medicines that I need to know about?

6. Are there any dietary modifications needed?

7. Are there any allergic factors involved? If so, do we need to test for them?

8. Will the condition cause any permanent scarring?

9. What symptoms would warrant our needing to see an allergist or a dermatologist?

10. When do I call you back if I do not feel the condition is improving adequately?

11. When do you wish to see my child again for this condition?

Eye Infection (*Conjunctivitis*)

Inflammation of the outer lining of the eye.

This is the condition that is commonly called "pink eye." There are several types, i.e. bacterial, viral, allergic and chemical. In the contagious types, usually your child only has to be isolated for a day or two once appropriate therapy begins.

1. What causes this condition, and how did my child acquire it?

2. Will this condition cause any permanent damage to the eyes?

3. How is it treated, and for how long?

4. If medicines are used, are there any potential side effects that can occur?

5. How long does it take to get over this condition?

6. Is this condition contagious and, if so, for how long?

7. When should we call you back if we don't think the medicine is working?

8. When do you wish to see my child again for this condition?

Eyelid Gland Swelling *(Chalazion)*

An inflammatory eyelid mass.

Most of these eyelid swellings get better on their own over a period of time, but sometimes this just does not happen. Keep in touch with your child's doctor regarding treatment. Generally, this condition does not cause any harm.

1. What causes this condition, and how did my child contract it?

2. How painful does it get?

3. Can it damage the eye or eyelid?

4. What other problems or dangers does it pose?

5. What is the treatment, and do antibiotics help?

6. If medicines are prescribed, what are their potential side effects and how long should they be taken?

7. How long does it take for this condition to resolve?

8. Will surgery ever be needed?

9. Do we need to consult an ophthalmologist?

10. When do you wish to see my child again for this condition?

Eye Muscle Imbalance *(Strabismus)*

Faulty alignment of the eye, secondary to eye muscle imbalance.

You need to see a pediatric ophthalmologist for this condition. The nice thing to know is that it is usually correctable.

1. What is the cause of this condition?

2. Will it correct itself, or will surgery be required?

3. Is there any other treatment for this condition other than surgery?

4. Does it affect the vision? If so, will the vision return to normal with treatment?

5. When do we need to see an ophthalmologist, and are there ones that specialize in this condition?

6. When do you wish to see my child again for this disorder?

Failure to Thrive

Not gaining weight or growing adequately.

This is a complicated condition to sort out . . . there can be some underlying medical disorder going on, but at times, no such cause is definable. In addition to your child's doctor, other specialists and caretakers frequently need to be involved. It is important that your child be followed closely until the condition is resolved.

1. What is the cause of this condition?

2. What diagnostic tests are necessary to further define what is going on?

3. What is the proposed treatment?

4. What are the potential problems that result from this condition, and what is the long-term outlook for my child?

5. Do we need to consult with any specialists regarding this condition?

6. Does the diet need to be modified?

7. What kind of follow-up is indicated?

8. When do you wish to see my child again regarding this condition?

Fainting *(Syncope)*

Fainting episode.

This may not be as prevalent a condition today as it was during your grandmother's time. Nonetheless, it still does happen and poses a danger for children actively engaged in an activity. Your child's doctor needs to be contacted and will likely establish guidelines for you to follow.

1. What is the cause of this condition?

2. Can this condition cause any long-term problems?

3. What tests need to be performed to establish the cause?

4. What safeguards do I need to employ to prevent it from happening again?

5. If it does occur, what steps do I take to ensure that my child will not be injured?

6. Is there any medicine that we can use that would be of help?

7. Do we need to consult with a specialist, such as a cardiologist or neurologist?

8. What signs shall I look for at home that might be considered alarming and that would indicate that I need to contact you?

9. When do you wish to see my child again regarding this condition?

Fifth Disease

An infectious skin disease characterized by reddened cheeks and lacy, flat, pink lesions on the surfaces of the trunk and extremities.

The most important fact to know about this condition is that once the rash appears, the child is no longer contagious. The contagious period takes place before the onset of the rash. The rash itself will usually disappear in two to three weeks, and the child may return to normal activities during this period of time.

1. What causes this condition, and how did my child contract it?

2. Is it contagious and, if so, for how long?

3. What complications can develop as a result of it?

4. How long will the rash last, and what other symptoms can occur?

5. What is the treatment, and what restrictions need to be imposed?

6. How long is the disorder contagious, and when can normal activities be resumed?

7. What dangers does this disease pose for people who have been exposed?

8. What kind of follow-up will be needed?

Flattened Head *(Positional Plagiocephaly)*

Flattened back of head.

For the most part, this is a by-product of having babies sleep on their backs, which the Academy of Pediatrics strongly recommends because it reduces the incidence of SIDS. Most of the time the condition is not serious enough to warrant any treatment other than an attempt to reposition the infant's head when lying down. Sometimes, however, it warrants the consideration of a corrective helmet, which is a judgement call on the part of your child's doctor.

1. What is the cause of this condition?

2. Is it correctable and, if so, how?

3. Will it cause any long-term problem for the brain or in the overall mental development?

4. What tests need to be done to further define this condition?

5. Should we see a craniofacial surgeon for this condition and, if so, when?

6. Considering this condition, should my child be permitted to sleep on his/her tummy and will it be of benefit in correcting the deformity?

7. If no treatment whatsoever is employed, what are the chances that this condition will correct itself and my child will grow up normally?

8. What kind of follow-up will be needed with you in the future regarding this condition?

Flu *(Influenza)*

An acute respiratory illness characterized by congestion, sore throat, red eyes, dry cough, fever, chills and achiness.

This condition causes doctors' offices to be packed during the winter months and accounts for many school absences. Fortunately, the flu vaccine offers good protection against the common strains of flu each year and has little side effects. For those who are unlucky enough to contract the flu, there are now new medicines that can shorten the course of this illness, if started early.

1. What causes this condition, and how did my child contract it?

2. What is its normal expected course?

3. Is it contagious, and how is it spread?

4. How long is the condition contagious, and when can my child resume activities?

5. What tests need to be done to more fully establish the diagnosis?

6. Is there any treatment that can be done to shorten the course of the disease or make it less severe?

7. Are there any potential side effects from the proposed treatment?

8. What symptoms or signs should I look for in my child that would necessitate my calling you back?

9. When do you wish to see my child again regarding this condition?

Foreign Body Aspiration

The breathing in of a foreign body into the
respiratory tract.

*This is a frightening experience when it happens to your
child, and if the child does not cough up the foreign body on
his/her own, it requires emergency action. At all one-year
check-ups, I tell every mom to avoid popcorn, peanuts,
unpeeled grapes, or unpeeled hot dogs until age four, as these
are common foods that infants can choke on and aspirate.*

1. What are the problems created by this?

2. How dangerous is it?

3. How do we plan to remove the foreign body, and is
    there any urgency to do it?

4. Are there any dangers in attempting to get the
    foreign body out?

5. Should we consult a specialist and, if so, when?

6. Has any permanent damage occurred as a result of
    the foreign body?

7. How can we prevent this from happening again?

Ganglion

A cyst of the tendon outer covering.

Children develop these lumps over their bones. They are totally safe, but at times can be painful. When one appears, the hope is that it will disappear on its own, but if it does not, the child may need to see a skilled orthopedist (bone doctor).

1. What causes this condition to occur?

2. Is it dangerous, and can it develop into something else?

3. Do any tests need to be performed to further aid in the diagnosis or treatment?

4. What are the options for treatment of this condition, and do we need to see an orthopedist (bone doctor)?

5. What limitations does this condition impose upon my child's activities?

6. What kind of follow-up is needed at your office concerning this condition?

Hair Loss *(Alopecia)*

It is important that your child sees the doctor to establish the cause for the hair loss. Most of the time the hair loss is temporary or correctable, but at times, it is necessary to see a dermatologist (skin doctor) who specializes in this type of condition.

1. What causes this condition?

2. What tests should be done to establish the cause?

3. Is the condition contagious?

4. Will it get worse?

5. Could there be a psychological cause for this disorder?

6. Will the hair grow back and, if so, over what period of time?

7. Assuming the hair grows back, will it be of the same thickness and consistency as before?

8. Are there any medicines to be used and, if so, for how long?

9. Are there any side effects that might be anticipated from these medicines?

10. Do we need to see a specialist for this condition?

11. When do you wish to see my child again regarding this disorder?

Hand Foot Mouth Syndrome

A condition characterized by reddened, blister-like eruptions on the hands, feet and mouth.

This viral syndrome gets better on its own, but sometimes causes considerable discomfort, especially if there are mouth lesions present. Paradoxically, not all children with this disease develop lesions in the mouth.

1. What causes this condition, and how did my child contract it?

2. Is it contagious and, if so, for how long?

3. What is the natural course for this condition, and what complications can occur?

4. Is there any treatment that needs to be employed?

5. What types of restrictions need to be imposed on my child's activities?

6. How long does this illness last?

7. What can I do to make my child feel better?

8. When do you wish to see my child again for this condition?

Hay Fever *(Allergic Rhinitis)*

An allergic condition characterized by runny nose and watery eyes that is frequently chronic and seasonal.

This condition seems to be occurring with greater frequency in the pediatric population, possibly secondary to the increasing pollution in our environment. Fortunately, in recent years there are good medicines available that can control the symptoms and cause little side effects.

1. What causes this condition, and how did my child develop it?

2. What medicines should my child use to treat it?

3. What are the side effects of these medicines?

4. Is there anything we can do in our home environment to make this condition better?

5. How long will this condition last?

6. What complications can my child develop from this condition?

7. Is this an allergic condition and, if so, how long should we wait to see an allergist?

8. When do I call you back regarding my child's progress?

9. Will you need to see my child again regarding this condition?

Headaches

This is a very common complaint in the pediatric population. It is important that you consult your child's doctor to rule out any serious underlying condition if the headaches persist or occur with significant frequency.

1. What is the cause of my child's headaches?

2. Are we sure that they are not a symptom of something more serious going on in the head?

3. Are there more tests that need to be performed to better define the cause of this disorder?

4. What medicine(s) should we use to treat the headaches?

5. What are the potential side effects of these medicines?

6. Is it important to have the eyes checked?

7. What symptoms do I look for to make sure the condition is not evolving into something more serious?

8. How long do I wait to call you back if the symptoms persist?

9. When would we need to see a neurologist?

10. When do you wish to see my child again regarding this condition

Head Lice

Parasitic insects that infect the hair and scalp, causing red areas and itching.

This condition is repugnant to most parents. It exists at times in epidemic proportions, especially in schools and daycare centers. In some children, the condition is resistant to some of the conventional therapies, but your doctor, I'm sure, will find a treatment that will kill even the most resistant of bugs.

1. What causes this condition, and how did my child contract it?

2. What is the treatment, and how effective is it?

3. Are there any potential side effects of the treatment?

4. How will I know if all the lice have been killed following the institution of treatment?

5. What advice should be given to people who have been recently exposed to my child?

6. How contagious is this condition, and when is my child no longer contagious?

7. How much school should my child miss as a result of this condition?

8. When do you wish to see my child again regarding this disorder?

Hearing Deficit

Diminished hearing.

This condition needs to be detected early and, if it persists, needs to be fully checked out and, if possible, corrected. It is thought by many that hearing problems in young infants left untreated can lead to learning difficulties later on. Fortunately, many nurseries now screen their newborns to rule out hearing loss.

1. What causes this condition?

2. Was my child born with this condition, or was it acquired?

3. What tests need to be performed to further delineate the cause and severity?

4. Is there any treatment for this disorder?

5. Is the condition correctable?

6. Has my child's learning process been affected?

7. Does my child need to see an ENT physician or an audiologist?

8. When do you wish to see my child again for this condition?

Heart Murmur

An abnormal heart sound.

Heart murmurs are very common in childhood. If they are of the innocent type, which means there is no structural abnormality, there is nothing to worry about. The organic type of murmur signifies some structural abnormality, which may be problematic for the child. Sometimes it is difficult for even the most skilled physician to be able to distinguish between the two with stethoscope alone. These children often need further investigation, sometimes from a pediatric cardiologist (heart specialist).

1. What causes this condition?

2. What is its significance?

3. What are the problems that can result because of it?

4. How is it treated?

5. What problem signs should I look for as a result of this condition?

6. Is there a possibility that this condition will resolve itself without treatment?

7. Will antibiotics be needed as a preventative to infection with future dental procedures?

8. Do we need to see a cardiologist?

9. When do you wish to see my child again for this condition

Heart Rhythm Irregularities *(Arrhythmias)*

Abnormal rhythm of the heartbeat.

Some heart rhythm abnormalities cause no harm to the child whatsoever, while others can be life threatening. Fortunately, these are rare, but they do exist, and warrant close medical scrutiny.

1. What causes this condition, and what problems does it pose for my child?

2. What tests need to be done to better define it?

3. What danger signs do we need to look for?

4. What is the treatment for this condition?

5. If medicines are to be used, what are their potential side effects?

6. What precautions, if any, need to be taken with regard to limiting exercise, diet, and everyday activities?

7. Do we need to see a cardiologist and, if so, when?

8. When do you wish to see my child again regarding this condition?

Hepatitis

Inflammation of the liver.

Many cases of hepatitis contracted during childhood go unde-tected and get passed off frequently as some non-specific virus because the child never becomes yellow (jaundiced). By receiv-ing Hepatitis A and B vaccines, which are given routinely in many pediatric offices, the chances of contracting this disease is minimized.

1. What causes this condition, and how did my child contract it?

2. What diagnostic tests need to be performed to establish the cause?

3. What are the dangers or complications that are associated with this condition and are they potentially preventable?

4. Is this condition curable, and will there be any long-term liver damage?

5. What is the treatment?

6. Are there any specific dietary or exercise restrictions?

7. Is the condition contagious and, if so, what steps need to be implemented to prevent its spread?

8. Does any person coming into contact with my child need to receive any specific treatment or vaccination?

9. What signs or symptoms would warrant my calling you back?

10. When do you wish to see my child again regarding this condition?

Hernia *(Inguinal)*

A weakness in the supporting tissues of the groin area, permitting the abdominal contents to bulge out.

This somewhat common surgical problem can be easily repaired by a competent surgeon who deals with pediatric patients. Most children experience little discomfort following the surgery.

1. What is the cause of this condition, and how did my child develop it?

2. What are the problems that can occur as a result of this disorder?

3. What are the options for treatment?

4. What are the potential complications of the proposed treatment?

5. What is the natural course of this condition if left untreated?

6. If surgery is indicated, when should it occur, where, and by whom?

7. When do you wish to see my child again for this condition?

Hip Joint Inflammation *(Synovitis)*

An inflammation of the lining of the hip joint.

This condition in childhood can cause severe pain in the hip joint when there is movement, and can be an alarming symptom for the parents to observe. Fortunately, this condition usually resolves on its own, typically within a week, and there is no residual damage. However, other, more serious, causes for the hip pain need to be ruled out by your child's doctor.

1. What causes this condition?

2. What complications can develop as a result of it?

3. How long will the symptoms persist?

4. What tests are needed to substantiate the diagnosis? Are x-rays needed?

5. What is the treatment for this condition?

6. Is this condition contagious?

7. What activities and exercise restrictions should be imposed, and for how long?

8. Is there any need to see an orthopedist and, if so, when?

9. What symptoms would warrant my calling you back?

10. When do you wish to see my child again regarding this condition?

Hydrocele (of the Testes)

Fluid in the scrotum surrounding the testicle.

This condition, which frequently presents at birth, can either resolve on its own or require surgical intervention and repair. Your child's doctor will be able to differentiate which type of hydrocele it is and whether your child will need to see a surgeon.

1. What causes this condition?

2. What is the natural course of this disorder?

3. What is the treatment for this condition, and is surgery ever indicated?

4. What are the potential complications that can occur as a result of the treatment?

5. If surgery is indicated, where, when, and by whom should the procedure be performed?

6. What are the chances of this condition resolving on its own without outside intervention?

7. What signs or symptoms would warrant my calling you back regarding this condition?

8. When do you wish to see my child again for follow-up?

Hypertension

High blood pressure.

High blood pressure, though rare, is always a worrisome finding in children and should be evaluated for an underlying cause before instituting a treatment plan. A blood pressure reading should always be a routine part of your child's yearly physical exam. [NOTE: A blood pressure cuff that is too small for a larger arm (often seen during adolescence) can give an artificially high blood pressure reading.]

1. What causes this condition?

2. What potential problems can it lead to?

3. What tests are needed to better understand why this condition has occurred?

4. Is it curable?

5. What medicines are used to treat this disorder, and what can we hope to accomplish with this treatment?

6. What are the side effects of the medicines?

7. Are there any other ways to control the blood pressure?

8. What are the long-term effects of this condition?

9. What restrictions in diet, exercise, and daily activities need to be imposed?

10. Are there any danger signs we need to look for that might indicate a complication of this disorder?

11. Should we consult a specialist in this type of disorder, and, if so, when?

12. When do you wish to see my child again regarding the high blood pressure?

Ingrown Toenail

A condition where the toenail grows into the flesh of the surrounding skin.

This condition is an argument for good fitting shoes and for cutting toenails straight across, as opposed to in a curvilinear fashion.

1. What causes this condition?

2. What is the treatment?

3. Can there be any complications from the treatment?

4. If surgery is indicated, will it be painful?

5. Do we need to see an orthopedist or a podiatrist?

6. What can we do to prevent this condition from recurring again?

7. When do you wish to see my child again regarding this condition?

Insect Bite

Symptomatic treatment is the treatment of choice for most of these occurrences, unless you suspect that the bite came from a poisonous critter. If so, consult with your child's doctor.

1. What can be done to relieve the symptoms caused from this bite?

2. Is there anything needed to prevent it from getting infected?

3. (In case of a spider bite) How do we know it is not a toxic spider bite?

4. (In case of a tick bite) How do we know that the bite is not from the type of tick that causes Lyme Disease?

5. What signs or developments would warrant our getting back in touch with you?

6. What kind of follow-up is needed?

ITP *(Idiopathic Thrombocytopenia Purpura)*

Small hemorrhages into the skin due to the deficiency of one of the blood clotting elements, not connected with any definable disease.

If you see little purple flat spots appear all over the body, they may represent small hemorrhages (petechiae) in the skin and warrant having your child seen by the doctor immediately.

1. What causes this condition, and how did my child contract it?

2. How long will it last, and is it completely curable?

3. What are the complications of this disorder?

4. Do we need to see a hematologist, and does my child need to be hospitalized?

5. What is the treatment for this disorder, and are there any potential side effects?

6. What kind of exercise limitations need to be imposed, and when will my child be able to resume a normal routine?

7. How often do we need to have follow-up blood tests?

8. When do you wish to see my child again for this disorder?

Kidney Infection *(Pyelonephritis)*

Infection of the kidneys.

This condition needs to be treated aggressively to totally eradicate the infection. It is of the utmost importance that you follow-up with your child's doctor. Further testing may be necessary to rule out any underlying structural abnormalities that could possibly lead to recurrent infections.

1. What is the cause of this condition, and how did my child contract it?

2. What complications can occur as a result of this condition?

3. What is the treatment?

4. What are the potential side effects of the treatment?

5. What diagnostic tests should be performed to determine any underlying structural cause?

6. Do we need to see a urologist?

7. Will there be any physical restrictions placed on my child because of this condition?

8. What symptoms would prompt me to call you back again?

9. What kind of follow-up will be needed to make sure this infection has been eradicated?

Laryngitis

Inflammation of the larynx.

Hoarseness is usually the most prominent symptom of this condition. One goal of the treatment plan should be to rest the voice. Most children, however, will have no part of this. You may have to rely on a good humidifier and possibly some prescription medicines to recover.

1. What causes this condition?

2. Is it contagious, and how is it spread?

3. What complications can possibly occur as a result of this disorder?

4. How is it treated?

5. If medicines are to be used, what side effects can occur?

6. How long will it take for my child to show improvement?

7. When can my child return to school and resume physical activities?

8. Will my child now be more prone to developing laryngitis on a recurrent basis?

9. What signs do we look for to make sure the condition is not getting worse?

10. When do you wish to see my child again for follow-up?

Learning Differences

It is important that you discuss concerns about your child's learning development and intellectual abilities with your doctor. Academic testing results and teachers' comments should also be funneled to the doctor's office. Often, the doctor can add another dimension to educational decisions that will affect your child.

1. What are the possible causes for this condition?

2. What can be done to remedy it?

3. How will my child be impacted educationally and career-wise from this condition?

4. Will my child need to attend remedial classes or a school that specializes in these kind of disorders?

5. How will my child be limited in the future in regards to activity participation?

6. What kind of follow-up is needed?

7. Do we need to see a specialist, such as an educational psychologist for further evaluation?

8. When do you wish to see my child again for this disorder?

Leg and Foot Structural Disorders
(i.e. Bowlegs, Knock Knees, Pigeon Toes, Flat Feet)

Many structural abnormalities that a generation ago were treated with braces and corrective shoes are now treated with watchful observation. Nonetheless, certain structural conditions do need orthopedic evaluation and corrective procedures, so always keep the doctor informed as to your concerns in this area.

1. What causes this condition?

2. Will it get worse?

3. Will the condition cause my child any pain or discomfort?

4. Is it correctable, or is it the type of condition that my child will outgrow without outside help?

5. Will the condition need corrective shoes or braces to correct the problem?

6. Should we consult an orthopedist or a podiatrist and, if so, when?

7. When do you wish to see my child again regarding this condition?

Lyme Disease

A condition characterized by skin eruptions, joint aches, and sometimes heart problems caused by a certain type of tick bite.

This condition, at times, is difficult to diagnose and is easily confused with many other disorders that have similar symptoms. It is important to make the diagnosis as early as possible in order to get the appropriate treatment and to prevent complications of this disease.

1. What causes this condition, and how did my child contract it?

2. What symptoms might we expect to see during the natural course of this disorder?

3. What are the complications that can occur?

4. How long will my child be affected by this disease?

5. What treatment can be employed?

6. Are there any side effects from the treatment, and is the treatment always successful?

7. What period of time will my child need to be out of school, and what kind of activity restrictions will need to be imposed?

8. What can we expect as a long-term outcome from this disorder?

9. Do we need to consult a specialist and, if so, when and what kind?

10. What symptoms would warrant getting back in touch with you immediately?

11. What kind of follow-up will be needed in the future?

Lymph Node Enlargement *(Lymphadenopathy)*

Enlarged lymph nodes (glands).

Swollen glands in the neck are a common finding in many children. Nonetheless, if you notice the sudden presentation of swollen glands or the glands appear larger than you think they should be, it is advisable to have the condition evaluated by the doctor for some possible underlying disease.

1. What causes this condition, and how did my child develop it?

2. What tests need to be performed to better delineate this disorder?

3. Can this condition lead to something more serious?

4. What is the treatment for this disorder?

5. If medicines are to be used, what side effects can occur?

6. How long can we expect the lymph nodes to remain enlarged?

7. Are there any complications that we should look for?

8. When do you wish to see my child again regarding this disorder?

Meningitis

Inflammation of the lining of the brain caused by infection.

This disease, if caused by a bacteria, can be devastating and requires aggressive medical treatment. Fortunately, we see a lot less of it since the routine administration of the Hemophillus Influenzae and Pneumococcal vaccines. Meningitis caused by a virus is usually much less serious.

1. What causes this condition, and how did my child contract it?

2. How serious is it?

3. Is it contagious and, if so, for how long and how is it spread?

4. What is the treatment, and is hospitalization necessary?

5. Are there any side effects to the treatment?

6. Do we need to consult an infectious disease specialist?

7. What advice should be given to people who have had recent contact with my child?

8. Will this condition cause any long-term residual effects?

9. When will my child be able to resume normal activities?

10. What kind of follow-up is needed?

Menstruation Onset *(Menarche)*

The onset of menstruation.

Most teenage girls think they know all about menstruation before it happens. Once it actually occurs, however, they may have a lot of questions, and the doctor's office is a good place to get answers.

1. What is the best way to explain to my child what is happening to her body?

2. What do I tell her to be aware of, and what things does she need to know specifically to aid in her hygiene?

3. How do I help her deal with the psychological aspects of this developmental stage?

4. Are there any available teaching aids or films that are available that may further help her in her understanding?

5. Should I expect any personality changes?

6. What type of regularity of menstrual period should be expected during the early months of menarche?

7. Is there anything that you personally might want to talk to her about?

8. When do you think it would be appropriate for her to see a gynecologist?

Mole *(Pigmented Nevus)*

A pigmented blemish of the skin.

Moles are a common finding in the general pediatric population. Nonetheless, a mole that changes in character or is painful should be brought to the attention of the doctor.

1. Is this condition in any way dangerous?

2. What is the possibility that it might become malignant?

3. What changes would I look for that might indicate something worrisome is occurring?

4. What would warrant the consideration of removing it?

5. Do we need to see a dermatologist?

6. What kind of follow-up is needed for this condition?

Mononucleosis

An acute, usually self-limited viral disease characterized by fever, fatigue, swollen tonsils, enlarged lymph nodes and, sometimes, enlargement of the spleen.

This condition, at one time, was referred to as the "kissing disease," but we know that it can be spread in ways other than the transfer of human saliva. It is very common in teens and needs close follow-up with the doctor. Generally, it takes quite awhile for the child's energy to fully return.

1. What causes this condition, and how did my child contract it?

2. What complications of this condition should I watch for?

3. Are there any medicines used to treat the disease?

4. Should the use of steroids be considered to shrink the size of the tonsils and make my child feel better?

5. How long is the condition contagious, and what type of quarantine regulations need to be imposed?

6. How is it transmitted, and how long does the illness last?

7. How long does my child need to stay completely away from all physical exercise, and what is the timetable for resuming activities and returning to school?

8. What advice should be given to people who have been recently in contact with my child?

9. Can this condition recur or become chronic?

10. When do you wish to see my child again for follow-up?

Mood Disorder
(i.e. Depression, Anxiety, Manic State)

These types of disorders seem to be occurring with increasing frequency in pediatric practices. If you suspect your child has a mood disorder, discuss it with the doctor. These conditions, if severe and left untreated, can be quite disruptive to a child's happiness and family life.

1. Why do children experience this type of disorder?

2. How serious do you think this disorder is?

3. Is it genetic or environmentally acquired?

4. How can I tell whether this is a phase or a long-term condition?

5. What can I do as a parent to make it better?

6. Does the condition warrant consulting a psychiatrist or psychologist?

7. Is there any medicine that can be used to improve this condition and, if so, are there any side effects?

8. When do you wish to see my child again for this condition?

Mouth Infection *(Stomatitis)*

Inflammation of the mouth.

This condition can be very unpleasant and painful for a child. A parent has to be quite resourceful in employing a treatment program that affords the child some comfort and relief.

1. What is the cause of this condition, and how did my child contract it?

2. Is it contagious and, if so, for how long?

3. How is it spread?

4. What is the treatment, and how effective is it?

5. Are there any side effects that can occur from the treatment?

6. What can be done to relieve the symptoms?

7. Can this condition recur and, if so, are there any ways to prevent it?

8. When do I call you back if the condition does not seem to be getting better?

9. When do you wish to see my child again regarding this illness?

Neck Muscle Contraction *(Torticolis)*

A contracted state of the neck muscle producing twisting of the neck.

This condition is frequently seen in early infancy. Parents should follow the exercises that the doctor prescribes to treat this condition, even though the exercises are unpleasant for the infant. If treated, you seldom see an older child with a residual problem from this condition.

1. What is the cause of this condition, and how did my child develop it?

2. What kind of treatment is indicated and how effective is it?

3. Can we expect a total correction of the condition and, if so, over what period of time?

4. Do we need to see a surgeon or a physical therapist for this condition?

5. What kind of follow-up is needed?

Nephritis

Inflammation of the kidney frequently characterized by blood in the urine.

This condition can possibly lead to progressively more impaired kidney function. It needs close and sustained follow-up with the child's physician.

1. What causes this disorder, and how did my child contract it?

2. What are the potential complications or dangers associated with this condition?

3. What tests are needed to further determine the cause of this disorder?

4. Is there any specific treatment and, if so, are there any potential side effects associated with the treatment?

5. Is exercise harmful with this condition?

6. Will there be any long-term kidney damage?

7. Do we need to see a nephrologist and, if so, when?

8. Are there any restrictions — physical, dietary, or otherwise — to be imposed upon my child that might aid in the recovery process?

9. What features should I look for that would warrant my calling you back?

10. When do you wish to see my child again regarding this condition?

Nosebleeds

This is a condition that can occur in clusters and usually resolves spontaneously on its own. If your child gets frequent nosebleeds, check with the doctor because there can be an underlying problem.

1. What causes this condition?

2. Can nosebleeds be dangerous?

3. Can my child become anemic from the loss of blood?

4. What can I do to treat the nosebleeds when they occur?

5. What can be done to prevent the nosebleeds from recurring?

6. Do we need to see an ENT specialist and, if so, when?

7. When do you wish to see my child again regarding this condition?

Obesity

Overweight.

This is a challenging problem. Children today are three times more likely to be obese than they were forty years ago. The problem is multi-faceted, and the treatment must come with the family working closely with the physician and possibly other specialists.

1. What are the likely factors that contribute to my child's weight problem?

2. Are there any tests that need to be done to explore the possibility of an underlying cause?

3. What are the potential problems and complications that this condition can cause for my child in the future?

4. What can be done to help correct the problem?

5. Is there anything that we, as parents, should do?

6. Do you think we should consult a specialty clinic, psychologist, or dietician?

7. What kind of follow-up will be needed in the future?

Pityriasis Rosea

A condition of the skin characterized by pink, scaly, plaque-like lesions often on the back, legs, arms and thighs.

This is an unattractive skin condition that fortunately goes away on its own with no specific treatment.

1. What causes this condition, and how did my child contract it?

2. Is it contagious, and how is it spread?

3. What is the natural course of this disease?

4. Will the lesions move to the face?

5. What do I do to treat it?

6. Are there any potential side effects from the treatment?

7. How long will it take for the lesions to disappear?

8. Under what conditions do I call you back

9. When do you wish to see my child again for a follow-up?

Pneumonia

Infection of the lungs.

This condition can be a serious problem. However, most children recover completely within one to two weeks, with close medical supervision and appropriate antibiotic therapy, assuming they have normal immune systems. Keep in close communication with the doctor and be sure to return for follow-up exams.

1. What causes this condition, and how did my child contract it?

2. What are the dangers associated with this condition?

3. Is it contagious and, if so, for how long?

4. Is there a need to obtain a chest x-ray?

5. What medicines are used to treat the condition?

6. What are the potential side effects of the medicines?

7. Once medicines are started, how long will it take for my child to show signs of improvement?

8. What should I look for that might indicate that the condition is getting worse?

9. Under what conditions should I call you back?

10. When can my child resume activities and return to school?

11. When do you wish to see my child again concerning this condition?

Poison Ivy

A type of skin rash that comes from contact with a specific plant with three leaves and usually causes itching and burning.

Some children contract this condition over and over again and require rounds of treatment every time. There is no vaccine to prevent poison ivy. The best advice I can give is find out where the poison ivy plant is and keep your child away from it.

1. How did my child contract poison ivy?

2. How is it treated?

3. What, if any, are the side effects of the treatment?

4. When can I expect the symptoms to improve and the rash to disappear?

5. Can it spread from person to person?

6. Will the clothes and linen that touch my child's skin need to be washed?

7. What can be done to prevent it from occurring again?

8. Will there be any residual scarring?

9. When can my child return to normal activities?

10. What kind of follow-up is needed?

Psoriasis

A chronic skin disease characterized by inflammation and silvery scaly patches.

This condition is more common than we would like to think. Most cases are mild, but some are severe and can be quite disfiguring. The latter type is more likely to be treated by a dermatologist (skin specialist).

1. What causes this condition?

2. What is the natural course of this disorder?

3. What is the treatment, and are there any potential side effects?

4. Does ultraviolet light help and, if so, is it safe for children?

5. What complications can occur as a result of this disorder?

6. Will there be any personal disfigurement?

7. Is there a specialist we need to see for this condition?

8. When should I call you back?

9. When do you wish to see my child again concerning this condition?

Pyloric Stenosis

An enlargement and tightening of the muscle in the lower stomach leading to obstruction with forceful vomiting.

This condition, characterized by projectile vomiting in infancy, is quite frightening for young parents. But actually, the required surgery to correct this condition is a very simple procedure by a competent pediatric surgeon and, barring any unforeseen complications, the recovery time is short.

1. What causes this condition, and how did my child develop it?

2. What are the potential complications that can occur from this disorder?

3. What tests are needed to substantiate the diagnosis?

4. What is the standard treatment of this disorder?

5. What are the potential complications of the treatment?

6. Will there be any residual problems following the proposed treatment?

7. What if we don't do anything — is there a chance that this condition will resolve on its own?

8. What kind of follow-up is needed?

Rheumatoid Arthritis — Juvenile

A condition characterized by chronic inflammation of the joints and surrounding tissue leading, at times, to chronic deformities.

This condition can cause much discomfort and pain during childhood and, in severe cases, can lead to chronic disability. It requires that the family work closely with the doctor to establish a treatment regimen that works.

1. What causes this condition?

2. Is it genetic?

3. What are the complications that can occur as a result of this condition?

4. What treatment can be used?

5. Are there any potential side effects from the treatment?

6. What criteria do we use to judge if the treatment is working?

7. Is there anything we can do to prevent long-term complications from this disorder?

8. Do we need to see a rheumatologist (arthritis specialist)?

9. What circumstances would require me to call you concerning my child's condition?

10. When do you wish to see my child again regarding this disorder?

Ringworm of Body *(Tinea Corporus)*

A fungal infection of the body.

This condition can be easily treated. The word "ringworm" refers to the round lesion with the elevated border, not an actual worm. You may have to be a good detective to find out what source the child came in contact with to contract this skin infection.

1. What is the cause of this condition, and how did my child contract it?

2. Is it contagious and, if so, for how long?

3. Do we need to contact the people with whom my child has been in contact?

4. How is it treated?

5. What are the potential side effects of the treatment?

6. How long will it take to clear up?

7. How do we prevent this condition from recurring?

8. Do we need to see a dermatologist?

9. When do you wish to see my child again for this condition?

Ringworm of Scalp *(Tinea Capitus)*

Fungal infection of the scalp.

This condition needs to be treated with oral medication. Creams by themselves will not clear it up. Fortunately, you don't have to shave your child's head and wear a beanie like they did in the old days.

1. What is the cause of this condition, and how did my child contract it?

2. Are there any tests that need to be done to better establish the cause?

3. What should we do to find the source?

4. Is it contagious and, if so, for how long?

5. Do we need to contact the people with whom my child has been in contact?

6. Does my child need to wear a cap or any other type of head covering?

7. What medication should be taken to treat this disorder and for how long?

8. Will the medicine cure the disease?

9. Are there any potential side effects from the medication?

10. When do we expect to see improvement?

11. Do we need to see a dermatologist?

12. When do you wish to see my child again for this condition?

Roseola

Baby measles.

When a child has roseola, it can be frightening for a parent, because there is typically a high fever for four-to-five days. The appearance of a rash at the end of the fever is almost a welcome relief, because it finally signifies to the doctor the true identity of the disease.

1. What causes this disease, and how did my child contract it?

2. What is the natural course of the disease?

3. Is it contagious and, if so, for how long?

4. When was my child first contagious?

5. Are there any complications that can occur as a result of this disease?

6. What is the treatment?

7. Should I notify people who have been in recent contact with my child and, if so, what advice should be given?

8. What limitations should be imposed on my child's activities during this illness?

9. Can my child contract this again in the future?

10. What kind of follow-up is needed?

Scabies

A skin disease caused by a mite and characterized by areas of inflammation on the skin and intense itching.

This disease is sometimes difficult to recognize in a child and gets confused with other skin conditions. Once recognized, however, it can be adequately treated. Because it is contagious, the school needs to be informed so they can be on the lookout for other children with the same condition.

1. What causes this condition?

2. What problems can be incurred as a result of scabies?

3. What is the treatment and how effective is it?

4. Are there any potential side effects of the treatment?

5. How long will it take for the rash to clear up?

6. How is it passed from one person to another, and how long will my child be contagious once appropriate treatment has begun?

7. Are there any long-term complications associated with this disorder?

8. When do you wish to see my child again regarding this condition?

School Phobia

Fear of going to school.

This condition can cause much frustration and fear on the part of the parent. The family should work closely with the doctor and other recommended specialists to help get through this problem area.

1. What is causing my child to act in this manner?

2. Is there anything that I, as a parent, am doing that is affecting the situation adversely?

3. Should I discuss the situation with the teachers and get them involved in the treatment program?

4. Are there any further diagnostic steps that need to be taken to uncover any possible underlying problems?

5. What else can be done to make this situation better?

6. Should we consult a psychologist or a psychiatrist?

7. What kind of follow-up will be needed with you?

Scoliosis

Curvature of the spine.

This condition needs to be followed closely by your child's doctor or a recommended orthopedic facility. Most children end up needing no treatment, but occasionally the condition will progress to the point where more aggressive therapy is needed.

1. What causes scoliosis?

2. Is it hereditary?

3. What is the natural progression of this disorder?

4. What symptoms can occur because of it?

5. How will this condition limit my child's participation in athletics?

6. What is the treatment for this disorder?

7. How often will x-rays be required to follow its progress?

8. Are there any exercises that can be performed to strengthen the back and to slow down the progression of this condition?

9. What role does surgery play in the correction of this disorder?

10. Do we need to be referred to a doctor or institution that specializes in this condition?

11. What kind of follow-up will be needed with you in the future?

Seizures

Convulsions.

These episodes are always very frightening. Fortunately, today there are newer medications available to treat the seizures that are quite effective when used by themselves or in combination with other medications under strict doctor's supervision. On the bright side, many children outgrow certain types of these convulsive disorders.

1. What causes seizures?

2. Can the type of seizures that my child has cause brain damage?

3. What tests are needed to better establish the cause?

4. What medicines are used to control the seizures?

5. How long will my child need to stay on these medicines, and what are their potential side effects?

6. Do we need to consult with a neurologist?

7. When do I need to call you back?

8. When do you wish to see my child again for this condition?

Sexual Abuse (Suspected)

If you suspect that this frightful event has occurred to your child, it is important that you contact the doctor's office as soon as possible. It is there that you will obtain the appropriate advice on where to go for examination and who to contact for proper documentation and follow-up.

1. How do I go about investigating whether an incident truly took place?

2. What type of proof do I need?

3. How do I make sure my child has not contracted any serious disease?

4. Do I need to remove my child from the suspicious environment?

5. What agency do I contact to report my suspicions and to help me investigate the situation?

6. Should my child be seen by any specific medical facility that could more legally substantiate my accusations or suspicions?

7. Should I have my child seen by a therapist, psychologist or psychiatrist?

8. Will you need to see my child again regarding this?

Sexually Transmitted Diseases *(STDs)*
(i.e. Gonorrhea, Syphilis, Herpes)

Whatever the specific disease might be, it needs to be diagnosed correctly and treated appropriately by a doctor. Counseling is definitely advised and partners should be sought out and treated if necessary.

1. What problems does this disease pose for my child?

2. How is it spread?

3. Can it be treated and cured with medicine? If so, how long will it take for my child to no longer be contgious?

4. How long after treatment begins will it take for this condition to completely get better?

5. What are the side effects of the medicine?

6. When will the symptoms disappear?

7. Will there be any permanent damage from this condition?

8. How should I counsel my child?

9. Does my child's sexual partner(s) need to be advised regarding this condition?

10. When do you wish to see my child again for this disease?

Short Stature

Excessive shortness in height.

This condition, especially in males, can have an adverse effect on the child's psyche. Your child's doctor can help by doing a complete work-up to rule out any underlying cause, such as growth hormone deficiency. Supplying information and giving reassurance is especially important to children who experience delayed puberty and are deemed to be "late bloomers."

1. What are the possible causes for this condition?

2. What diagnostic tests are needed to define the cause of the delayed growth?

3. If the tests indicate a problem, is there anything that can be done to help promote further growth?

4. After all the tests are done, will you be able to give me an estimation of the height that my child will eventually achieve?

5. Do we need to see an endocrinologist or any other specialist for an evaluation?

6. What suggestions can you give me so that I personally can help my child deal with this condition?

7. How often do you feel it is necessary for you to follow my child's growth in the future?

Sinusitis

Infection of the sinuses.

Symptoms of sinusitis in childhood may be vague and non-specific. There may be only a persistent cough and nasal congestion. The classic headache and green runny nose usually associated with sinusitis are not always present. Once the condition is diagnosed, however, it is important that a full treatment course be completed as this problem can recur over and over again.

1. What causes sinusitis, and how did my child develop it?

2. What diagnostic tests need to better define the condition?

3. How is it treated?

4. Are there any potential side effects from the treatment?

5. Can the disorder be possibly allergy related and, if so, what can be done about it?

6. Will an x-ray be needed at the end of the treatment to make sure the sinus infection is completely gone?

7. What can be done to prevent this condition from recurring in the future?

8. Do we need to see a specialist for this type of disorder?

9. When do you wish to see my child again for a follow-up?

Skin Infection *(Impetigo and Cellulitis)*

Superficial infection of the skin.

This condition is very common in childhood. Children are constantly getting scrapes and insect bites, which can then become infected. The high frequency of occurrence emphasizes the need for good handwashing techniques to be encouraged in all children.

1. What is the cause of this condition, and how did my child contract it?

2. Is it contagious and, if so, what can I do to prevent its spread?

3. What is the treatment for this condition?

4. Are there any side effects from the medicines used for the treatment that I should be aware of?

5. What advice should be given to people who have been in contact with my child?

6. Is this a type of disorder that can recur?

7. Are there potential complications from this disorder?

8. When should I see improvement in my child?

9. Do you need to see my child again for this condition?

Sleep Disorders
(i.e. Night Terrors, Nightmares, Difficulty Getting to Sleep, Sleepwalking)

These maddening conditions can lead to many sleepless nights on the part of the child and parents. Consult your doctor regarding any specific medication or behavioral modification that can be used.

1. What causes this sleep disorder?

2. What dangers are posed by this disorder?

3. What tests need to be done to better define this condition?

4. Is there any treatment indicated?

5. Are there any potential side effects that can occur from the treatment?

6. Do you suggest any adjustments in my family's lifestyle to treat this?

7. Will my child outgrow this condition and, if so, when?

8. Do we need to consult a specialist, such as a psychologist or sleep disorder clinic?

9. When do you wish to see my child again for this problem?

Small Head (Microcephaly)

Pediatricians measure the head circumference at every routine visit during the child's infancy to pick up conditions such as this. It is worrisome when a child's head is not growing adequately. Your child's doctor will advise you on what diagnostic tests are necessary and what to do next.

1. What causes this condition?

2. What are the future implications of this condition regarding learning and intellectual function?

3. What diagnostic tests are needed to further establish the cause and define the condition?

4. What is the proposed treatment for this condition, and how successful is it?

5. What specialist should we consult and when?

6. Are there any genetic implications that could affect future children we might have?

7. When do you wish to see my child again regarding this condition?

Spitting Up *(Gastroesophageal Reflux)*

Spitting up due to an incompetent "valve" that separates the stomach from the esophagus (swallowing tube).

This is one of the most common problems pediatricians deal with during the child's first year of life. Many medicines and formula changes might be tried at times with only variable success. The encouraging fact is that ninety percent of children outgrow this condition by the time they are eighteen months old.

1. What causes this condition?

2. What symptoms and complications can occur because of it?

3. How is this condition treated, and for how long?

4. How effective is the treatment and, if medicines are used, what are the potential side effects that can occur?

5. How do I guard against my child choking or aspirating when lying on the back?

6. What are the chances that my child will outgrow this disorder with or without treatment?

7. Do we need to be referred to a doctor who specializes in this condition?

8. What symptoms or signs would warrant my calling you back?

9. When do you wish to see my child again regarding this condition?

Sprain of Extremity
(i.e. Toe, Ankle, Knee, Finger, Wrist, Elbow)

The wrenching of a joint with partial rupture or other injury of its attachment.

This condition occurs often in childhood as children are frequently putting their bodies at risk in various forms of play or exercise. Consult your child's doctor when you suspect a sprain has occurred. Most of these conditions get better with rest alone, but some of the severe ones need orthopedic follow-up.

1. What is a sprain?

2. What is the treatment for this condition?

3. Are x-ray studies needed to make sure there is no fracture?

4. How long will the discomfort last?

5. What is the timetable for resuming activities that involve the injured part of the body?

6. Is there a possibility that there will be any permanent disability?

7. Do you think it is necessary to consult an orthopedist?

8. When should I bring my child back for a follow-up exam?

Stye

An inflammation of an eyelid gland.

This condition usually clears up with localized treatment. Realize, though, that the condition can progress and involve the entire eyelid, warranting more generalized treatment.

1. What causes a stye?

2. What complications can occur because of it?

3. How is it treated, and are antibiotics indicated?

4. What are the potential side effects of the treatment?

5. Are any isolation precautions necessary because of this condition?

6. How long does it take for this condition to resolve?

7. What signs would warrant my getting back in touch with you?

8. When do you wish to see my child again for this condition?

Tear Duct Obstruction (Nasolacrimal)

A blocked or partially blocked duct in the tear apparatus.

This condition causes recurrent discharge from the eye during the first months of life. It is a common occurrence during infancy. Most of the time the condition responds to a conservative treatment plan prescribed by your child's doctor. If not, the child may need to see an ophthalmologist (eye specialist) for further intervention.

1. What causes this condition?

2. What are the complications that might occur as a result of it?

3. Can the vision be affected in any way?

4. What is the treatment?

5. What are the chances for success as a result of the treatment?

6. What symptoms would warrant my contacting you again regarding this condition?

7. When do you wish to see my child again for reevaluation of this disorder?

Thrush

A fungal disease of infants characterized by whitish spots in the mouth.

This condition often looks worse than it actually is. Sometimes more than one round of medicine is needed to make it go away. Also, if you are a nursing mom, be careful! You might contract the infection on your breast.

1. What is the cause of this condition, and how did my child contract it?

2. Is it contagious and, if so, how is it spread?

3. Does it cause any discomfort during feeding?

4. Is there any problem with my child's immune system that may have led to the development of this condition?

5. What is the treatment for this disorder?

6. If medicines are used, are there any side effects to look for?

7. How long does it take for the condition to improve with treatment?

8. Can the condition spread to any other parts of the body?

9. If I am nursing my baby, is there any particular prescription to apply to my breasts to prevent my contracting this disorder?

10. What symptoms or signs would warrant my calling you back and when?

11. Do you wish to recheck my child for this condition?

Tonsilitis

Inflammation of the tonsils.

When your child complains of a sore throat, possibly accompanied by fever, you need to take the child to the doctor to have the throat cultured in order to rule out the possibility of strep. If the child has strep, you will receive medicine to treat the condition.

1. What causes tonsillitis?

2. Is it contagious and, if so, for how long?

3. What is the treatment for this condition?

4. Are there any side effects from the proposed treatment?

5. When can my child resume activities?

6. How many times does my child need to have this condition before a tonsillectomy is considered?

7. If the cause of this condition is strep, do you need to culture other family members and contacts?

8. What precautions need to be observed because of this condition?

9. What kind of follow-up is needed?

Torsion of the Testicles

Twisting of the testicle.

This condition is considered by some to be a pediatric emergency and, if suspected, warrants immediate diagnosis and treatment.

1. What is the cause of this condition, and how did my child develop it?

2. What potential problems can develop as a result of this disorder?

3. Are there any tests to be done to further define the problem?

4. What can be done to correct the problem?

5. Should we consult a surgeon now?

6. Is there a chance that my child will be sterile because of this condition?

7. What can be done to prevent it from occurring again?

8. What kind of follow-up is needed?

Tourette's Syndrome

A condition characterized by involuntary muscle spasms and vocal outbursts often associated with multiple erratic movements.

The nice thing you can say about this disturbing disorder is the tics that characterize this condition can be adequately treated in most cases and that these children can usually lead normal lives.

1. What is the cause of this condition?

2. How will it impact my child's lifestyle?

3. Is it genetic?

4. What is the treatment, and how effective is it?

5. What are the potential side effects of the treatment?

6. Does this disorder affect my child's learning abilities, and what limitations in activities should be imposed?

7. What is the usual long-term outcome for children with this condit ion?

8. Do we need to see a neurologist or psychiatrist?

9. What is the possibility of other siblings being affected with this disorder?

10. How should other siblings in the family be instructed to deal with and react to this child's disorder?

11. What should I tell the school?

12. When do you want to see my child again for this condition?

Umbilical Cord Stump Inflammation
(Umbilical Granuloma)

Persistent inflammatory remnant of the umbilical cord located at the base of the bellybutton.

This area of raw tissue in the infant's bellybutton can be easily treated in the office by your child's doctor, with no serious ill effects.

1. What is the cause of this condition, and how did my child develop it?

2. What treatment is needed, or will it heal by itself?

3. What are the potential side effects of the treatment?

4. Will it end up being cosmetically disfiguring in any way?

5. Are there any long-term complications from this condition?

6. Is there any follow-up needed?

Vomiting

This condition is a common experience in childhood and can lead to dehydration if it persists. It is wise to contact your child's doctor for information on how to treat the condition and to keep in close communication if the vomiting continues.

1. What is causing the vomiting?

2. How long should this condition last, and what problems can occur as a result of it?

3. Is the condition contagious and, if so, how is it spread?

4. What is the treatment for this condition?

5. If medicines are used, what are their potential side effects?

6. Is any further testing needed to establish the cause for the vomiting?

7. What symptoms do I look for to determine whether my child is becoming dehydrated?

8. Under what circumstances would I need to call you back?

9. What kind of follow-up is needed?

Part 3:

Choosing a Pediatrician

Choosing a pediatrician to take care of your new baby is one of the most important health care decisions you will ever make. Being on the same wavelength as your pediatrician is crucial for the best medical decision-making in the future. That's why I advise moms to make an appointment to meet prospective pediatricians during pregnancy.

The visit not only gives you an opportunity to meet the doctor, but to familiarize yourself with the workings of the practice. It is important that you like what you see, as you will probably be spending a great deal of time in this office once the baby arrives.

Use the interview to share your concerns and views. Be prepared with a list of questions on topics ranging from feeding to sleeping, vaccines, on-call procedures and other office practices. Here are some specific questions you might ask during the interview. I've compiled this list from questions my patients have asked me during interviews over the years.

1. Are you on my health plan and do you intend to stay on it?

2. How long have you been practicing pediatrics?

3. What are your office hours, and are after-hours and weekend visits available?

4. How are after-hours calls handled, and how long will I usually have to wait for a phone call to be returned? How accessible is the doctor if I want to speak directly to him or her?

5. Are you board-certified by the American Academy of Pediatrics?

6. Will you visit my baby in the hospital following delivery? Will the baby be examined every day during the hospital stay?

7. What is the normal wait time in your waiting room?

8. Do you schedule well checks and sick visits at separate times during the day or do you have other provisions for separating the sick children from the well ones.

9. Under ordinary circumstances, will I see you at each visit or will I be rotated to other doctors in the practice or a nurse practitioner?

10. What is your philosophy towards the use of antibiotics?

11. What is your philosophy regarding breastfeeding?

12. If my child has an emergency after hours or needs to be hospitalized, what hospitals do you use?

13. What doctors cover for you when you are unavailable? Will they have access to my child's records, and are they all on my insurance plan?

14. If your physician is not a pediatrician (e.g., she or he is a family doctor), how much training have you had in pediatrics and what pediatricians do you use for consultation in case of a serious illness?

In Closing

One of the most exciting things for me about being a pediatrician is having the privilege of being a trusted advisor to the family. The fact that I can play this role in the lives of people I come in contact with every day is very exciting and continually makes me look forward to being in the office.

I want every mom who comes to my office to leave feeling confident in her ability to cope with the illness at hand — indeed, that's why I wrote this book. But I also want every mom to know that babies don't break, and that it's just as important to relax and enjoy your child as it is to teach them to crawl or walk or read. Take time for yourself and your spouse. Nap when the baby is napping — it's age-old wisdom, but it's important. Raising kids isn't a sprint — it's a marathon. Pace yourself and enjoy the time you have with them. Eighteen years whizzes by in a flash, and you want to look back and remember that you enjoyed every minute of it. Thank you for letting me be a part of this important process.

— Gary C. Morchower, M.D.